OUR WORLD IN COLOUR

BANARAS

OUR WORLD IN COLOUR

BANARAS

Text by Shobita Punja

Photography by Pankaj Shah

The Guidebook Company Limited

Text by Shobita Punja
Photography by Pankaj Shah

Editors: Jonathan Griffin and David Clive Price
Series Editor: Caroline Robertson
Designed by De•Style Studio
Created by Gulmohur Press, New Delhi

The author and photographer would like to thank the Hotel Taj Ganges for their assistance in the production of this book.

Production House: Twin Age Ltd, Hong Kong

Printed in China

ISBN 962-217-268-7

Title spread
The ancient city of Banaras is one of the most important centres of pilgrimage or tirths for Hindus. It is also called Kashi, the City of Light. Over the centuries ghats or steps have been constructed to provide convenient access to the river for pilgrims and worshippers and also protect the banks from the eroding powers of the water.

Right
The sanctity of Banaras is derived from the river Ganga and Hindu mythology. It is said that Shiva, Lord of the Universe, was cleansed of the sin of murder when he bathed in the Ganga at Banaras. It is therefore the desire of all pilgrims to bathe and receive the same spiritual cleansing power of the river.

Pages 6-7
There are several bathing and cremation ghats at Banaras. The mushroom-shaped bamboo umbrellas are used by individual priests and devotees. On festive days the steps of the ghats teem with people.

Pages 8-9
Sarnath, near Banaras, is a famous Buddhist site associated with the first sermon preached by the Buddha. In the Buddhist lore Sarnath is referred to as the "deer park" for it was then a serene wooded forest. In sculpture there are depictions of Buddha delivering his sermon as the deer of the forest, forgetting their conventional shyness, come to hear the master speak.

Pages 10-11
Several grand festivals take place in Banaras throughout the year. The most spectacular performance, however, is the Ramlila, when the streets of Banaras come alive to the sounds of the ritual processions on elephants and the theatrical enactment of the story of Rama.

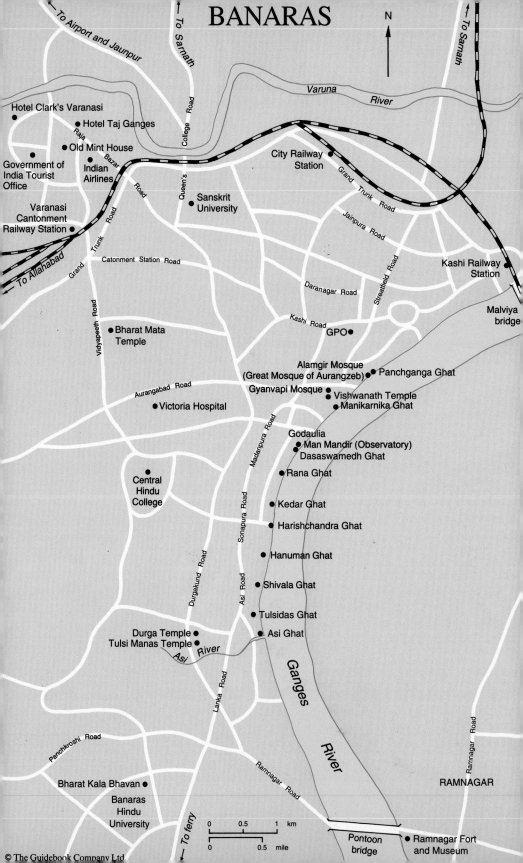

BANARAS

N

To Airport and Jaunpur
To Sarnath
To Sarnath

Varuna River

- Hotel Clark's Varanasi
- Hotel Taj Ganges
- Old Mint House

Raja

Bazar

Government of
India Tourist
Office

Indian
Airlines

Varanasi
Cantonment
Railway Station

Road

College Road

Queen's Road

- Sanskrit University

City Railway
Station

Grand Trunk Road

Jainpura Road

Kashi Railway
Station

Streatfield Road

Grand Trunk Road

To Allahabad

Catonment Station Road

Daranagar Road

Malviya
bridge

Vidyapeeth Road

Kashi Road

- GPO

- Bharat Mata
  Temple

- Alamgir Mosque
  (Great Mosque of Aurangzeb)
- Panchganga Ghat

Aurangabad Road

- Gyanvapi Mosque
- Vishwanath Temple
- Manikarnika Ghat

- Victoria Hospital

Madanpura Road

- Godaulia
- Man Mandir (Observatory)
- Dasaswamedh Ghat

- Central
  Hindu
  College

Sonapura Road

- Rana Ghat

- Kedar Ghat

- Harishchandra Ghat

- Hanuman Ghat

Durgakund Road

Asi Road

- Shivala Ghat

- Tulsidas Ghat

- Durga Temple
- Tulsi Manas Temple

Asi River

- Asi Ghat

Lanka Road

Ganges River

Panchkroshi Road

- Bharat Kala Bhavan

Banaras
Hindu
University

To ferry

Ramnagar Road

Ramnagar Road

RAMNAGAR

0   0.5   1 km

0   0.5   mile

Pontoon
bridge

- Ramnagar Fort
  and Museum

© The Guidebook Company Ltd

BANARAS, BENARAS AND VARANASI are some of the names of this holy Indian city. A city which, since it is both an exalted place of pilgrimage and an idealized centre of faith, has been likened to Jerusalem and Mecca. For the Hindu, Banaras has attained her sanctity and importance in manifold ways. Ancient mythology and legends have cast a veil over the city, making her one of the most intriguing places in the world. A long history of ruin and reconstruction have turned her into one of the most enduring cities of India. A city where eternity and continuity, the past and present live together.

The city of Banaras is situated on the west bank of the holiest of all Indian rivers, the Ganga or Ganges. The relationship between the sacred site on which the city was built and the river is the essence of Banaras. The Ganga is believed to have flowed from the heavens to wash away the ashes of the dead. In heaven, she is seen as the Milky Way that leads to the vast universe of immortality. According to the myth, the sage Bhagirath undertook a great penance to bring the Ganga down to earth. Shiva, the Lord of the Universe, was requested to bear the weight of the mighty river. As she cascaded from the heavens, the force of her waters lost their momentum in Shiva's locks and the trickles that descended to earth formed one of the world's great rivers.

In sacred literature the River Ganga is personified as a goddess, to be worshipped and respected. The river's course begins in the Himalayas. The holy sites of Haridwar and Rishikesh mark where she joins the plains. There are other sacred sites at confluences where tributary rivers meet the Ganga. In her 2,510-kilometre (1,568-mile) journey to the sea, the Ganga traverses the central plains of northern India. Moving from west to east, she meets the Brahmaputra toward the end of her journey and finally flows into the Bay of Bengal. The imagery of this mighty river is central to Hindu thought. The life of a human being is seen as a wave on the river that meanders until it ultimately loses itself in the great ocean of eternity, from where all life originates.

The great mosque of Banaras, built by Aurangzeb in the 17th century, overlooks the city and still dominates the skyline. Part of the daily ritual in temples and small shrines begins at dawn with priests waking the god, bathing the image with holy water and milk. Then the image is dressed with flowers, jewels and clothes. When the idol is ready the temple doors are opened so that the devotees can meet the god.

The River Ganga is 'the remover of affliction, the emancipator from the ocean of worldly existence'. Her presence at Banaras is vital to her story. The River Ganga is described in the sacred texts as a mother, for she has sustained life on the vast plains of India for centuries. She is remembered as 'a mother who holds her child to her bosom and cleanses the baby of excrement and dirt'. Her power to heal and console, to carry away spiritual dirt and emotional excrement is exemplified in another myth. The Great God Shiva, in one of his many exploits, lost his temper with Brahma, the Lord of Creation. In his anger, he cut off one of the five heads of Brahma. The severed head stuck to Shiva's hand, like the blood on Lady Macbeth's hands. Wandering the worlds, he could find no way of ridding himself of the skull of Brahma, or the sin that he had committed. Until he came to Banaras. Bathing in the Ganga, the skull just slipped away and Shiva was finally released from the burden of his guilt. Hindu's believe that if the Great God Shiva could be washed clean at Banaras, then there must also be salvation for humans and other forms of life. So it is that Banaras is known as the city of liberation and the city of Shiva.

A boat ride down the Ganga, at dawn or dusk, shows Banaras' strongest character and her intimate affiliation with the river. It is on the western curve of the river that the city was constructed. The name Varanasi is said to have derived from the two rivers, the Varana and the Asi, which meet here with the river Ganga and form the city's northern and southern boundaries. From the boat, or from the riverside, the skyline of Banaras stands tall and silent, dotted with temple spires, mosques and terraced buildings.

From the north the first city landmark is the Rajghat plateau, an ancient site with one of the oldest temples, the Adi Keshava, and one of the few shrines in Banaras dedicated to Vishnu. Further down the river the huge frame of the Malaviya Bridge looms across the waters. Built this century, the bridge now performs the task once undertaken by ferries that transported goods, livestock and people from one side to the other. As the boat moves further downstream the curve of the Ganges becomes visible and the great ghats present their angular profiles, catching the light and casting shadows over themselves. From out of her waters, high ramparts and stairs emerge from the western bank and, like the roots of an old tree, they appear to buttress the entire city. The propensity of the city to reach down and touch the river waters is exaggerated by the precarious position of some of the buildings and the constant overflow of people at the riverside taking their ritual bathes.

Mark Twain wrote of the spectacular riverside view of the city:

It is compactly walled from sight by this crammed perspective of platforms, soaring stairways, sculptured temples, majestic palaces, softening away into the distances; and there is movement, motion, human life everywhere, and brilliantly costumed, streaming in rainbows up and down the lofty stairways, and massed in metaphorical gardens in the miles of great platforms at the river's edge.

It is beside the holy waters of the Ganga that the activities for which Banaras is held sacred are performed. Everyday thousands of residents and pilgrims bathe, offer prayers to the elements, to the life-giving energy of the sun, and to their dead ancestors who have been carried away by these waters. What draws people to the river is a deep-rooted belief that these waters can cleanse the soul of the sins of many generations. Everyone has their own way of celebrating the ritual contact with the holy Ganga: some bathe; others dip themselves entirely into the water once, thrice or any number of times; some drink the water; others make water offerings to the sun; while others fill their pots with holy water to take back to their homes to perform rituals and purification. What can be offered to the waters that nurture such a variegated existence on earth? Pilgrims give flowers (the fragrance of their personality), fruits (of their labour), lamps (of knowledge) and

There are many ghats that have been built by different generations of donors.

their respectful prayers. On festival days and religious occasions the riverside is thick with their colourful offerings bobbing up and down on the waters.

The land around Banaras is also held sacred because Shiva is believed to have lived here. When the great Lord of the Universe was married to Parvati he first lived in her father's kingdom, the great abode of the Himalayan mountains. Lost in the clouds and frolicking midst the snows, Shiva and Parvati spent many god-years. Complaints reached the divine couple that the world was suffering because of Shiva's monumental neglect. He was asked to find some place on earth to live where human beings could find him should they need his help. Shiva selected Banaras as his new residence and he manifested himself there in many forms to serve the demands of all his devotees.

There are thousands of temples at Banaras dedicated to gods and goddesses-particularly to the deities of good fortune and prosperity-and to the sun and the planets. The most important are those that honour the several manifestations and attributes of Shiva. There is the Kashi Kedareshvara, the Field of Liberation, on the southern sector of the river bend, Omkareshvara, the Source of all Wisdom, and Mahakalaeshvara, the Lord of Great Time or Eternity, and so on.

The major shrine at Banaras is the Visvanatha Temple, devoted to Shiva as the Lord of the Universe. Popular explanations confer on Shiva the role of The Destroyer. In essence, the whole process of creation, preservation and death is seen as one, a continuity of the same phenomena. Hence Shiva as the Lord of All encompasses life as well as the thereafter. The Visvanatha Temple structure that stands today has been reconstructed many times. It houses a linga, a stone form that symbolizes his tumultuous creative energy. The shrine is open to Hindus only, though there are balconies and neighbouring parapets from which the interior of the temple can be seen.

This temple houses an image around which one of the most powerful myths of Hindu belief has been woven. The story begins with Vishnu, the Preserver of Life, resting on the ocean of eternity. Brahma, passing by, saw Vishnu lying there unconcerned by his presence. They began to fight, each accusing the other of disrespect. The other gods were perturbed by this and requested that Shiva intervene. Shiva then appeared as a great pillar of light, endless and infinite, like space. Vishnu and Brahma interrupted their quarrel to find out what this pillar of light was. Vishnu went off in search of the bottom of the pillar and Brahma explored the top. Neither of them could find the limits of the pillar of light. Shiva then revealed himself and explained his supremacy over the entire universe, of which he was the originator. He said everything is created from him and that all things will ultimately dissolve into him, like waves in the eternal ocean. The appearance of the pillar of light is said to have occurred at the site of the Visvanatha Temple. The holy city within Banaras is thus called Kashi 'The Luminous One' or the 'City of Light'.

Light in Hindu philosophy has great significance for it represents the wisdom that destroys the darkness of ignorance. Sin and evil are understood to be the acts of ignorance. When wisdom is acquired, evil will vanish. Sin cannot be washed away by water or prayer but only by wisdom. Immortality is also gained through wisdom. So the City of Light is the City of Eternal Wisdom as well. To die in the city beside the river of life is to die with a promise of salvation, a promise to be released from the endless cycle of life and death and reincarnation, and to gain *moksha* or eternal liberation. So for centuries thousands of people have come to Banaras to die and thousands have brought the ashes of the dead here to immerse them in the holy waters.

The sanctity of the city of Banaras is enhanced by the presence of the Ganga, the most sacred of India's rivers.

Along the water's edge, the burning ghats are cramped with funeral pyres. The most sacred Ghat is the Manikarnika, which is associated with the touch of the goddess, Shiva's wife. On the burning ghats, or cremation areas, wooden platforms are created on which the corpses are laid. A male member of the family, usually the heir, lights the pyre, thereby assuming responsibility for the rest of the family. If the family is rich, the pyre will be scented with fragrant sandalwood. Leaving the pyre to burn, the family returns home to bathe and cleanse themselves. It is believed that the soul of the dead takes some time to reach the 'other shore' and so the family is required to perform certain rituals to ensure that the soul is neither hungry nor wanting in courage. The rituals also serve to bond the family members in their days of sorrow. On the prescribed day, the family gives final release to the soul from its earthly existence. With promises to remember the dead, but not to hold on to them or to call them back, the family can now return to reconstruct their lives in the absence of their loved one.

Banaras forces one to reflect about life, to ponder about creation and the insignificance of temporal wealth in the face of death. The poverty, anguish and sadness that is visible on the face of Banaras is one of its most moving features. The

The gods of the Hindu pantheon are given an animal mount, a manifestation of their attributes. Shiva rides on a bull, the goddess Durga on a lion, the holy river goddesses Ganga and Yamuna ride on mythical creatures, the crocodile-like makara and the turtle respectively.

city is so intimately associated with death and thoughts about life and life after death, that sages, teachers, philosophers and poets of every sect and caste are drawn to her shore.

The Buddha was one such philosopher. He was born a prince, in the 6th century BC, in present-day Nepal. Abandoning his family, wife, child, palace and wealth, he wandered through the villages of north-eastern India in search of truth. The texts speak of his discussions with sages of all religions and denominations. It was at Bodh Gaya, in Bihar, that he attained enlightenment and found the meaning of life. From that time onwards he was called the Buddha, which means the Enlightened One. Having understood that desire, in any form, is the cause of all suffering, the Buddha was content to pass his life away. He wished for nothing-not fame nor fortune, not to teach, not for life itself. It was then that he came to the peaceful forest grove at Sarnath on the northern outskirts of Banaras. There in the deer park, a few disciples persuaded him to speak of his philosophy so that they may teach others. The Buddha consented and gave his first sermon. In so doing he founded the first Buddhist Sangha, or religious order. Sarnath has thus become a site associated with one of the world's greatest teachers and visiting it can be a moving experience. There one can see evidence of the simplicity and charm of his gentle philosophy. A philosophy that teaches respect for all forms of life and cautions men against satisfying their excessive greed at the expense of others.

Excavations at Sarnath have revealed ancient ruins of stupas and funeral mounds of Buddhist saints and teachers, as well as remains of monasteries. Buddha lived more than 500 years before Christ and the ruins of Sarnath suggest that it was an important place of pilgrimage, study and prayer for more than a thousand years. Most prominent among the buildings of Sarnath is the tall brick mound of the Dhamek stupa, almost 44 metres (143 feet) high. Believed to have been originally constructed by Emperor Ashok, a Buddhist convert, it was rebuilt in the Gupta period almost 800 years later, in the 5th century AD. The stupa is said to mark the spot where the Buddha gave his first address.

Excavations in 1904 unearthed beautiful polished stone pillars and sculptures that can now be seen in the museum at Sarnath. At the entrance to the museum is the huge polished stone capital of a free-standing pillar said to have been erected by Emperor Ashok in the 3rd century BC. The capital comprises four lions, seated back to back, facing out in four directions. This capital once had a huge wheel that was supported on the backs of the lions. Below the lions is a band of relief sculptures. There are four wheels, which are the symbols of the law of Dharma, of progress and movement. Between them are the figures of a bull, an elephant and a lion, symbols of devotion, strength, and power respectively, and the figure of a swift running horse. These symbols indicate the attitudes with which one should serve the cause of peace. The lion capital has been selected as the emblem of the Indian Republic; it heads all government documents and is stamped on every Indian coin and note.

The museum has some exquisite sculptures of the Buddha. He is depicted meditating under the Bodhi tree, the tree of wisdom and enlightenment, and, in capturing his peaceful expression, the sculptors reveal the eternal youthfulness of Buddha's ideas. Other depictions show Buddha presenting his first sermon in the deer park. His right hand is often lifted in blessing, offering protection, while a halo of light and wisdom radiates around him, distinguishing him above all others.

Banaras has always been associated with wisdom and philosophy. It was an ancient seat of learning and the Banaras Hindu University carries on this tradition. The University campus, to the south of the city, was constructed at the beginning of this century through the pioneering efforts of Pundit Madan Mohan Malaviya. During the colonial period, universities based on the British system of education were set up in Calcutta, Madras and Bombay. In 1905, Malaviya put forward the idea of creating a university that was more distinctly Indian and that would preserve the best of Indian culture, art and philosophy. The Maharaja of Banaras donated the land for the campus and the foundation stone of the Banaras Hindu University was laid by the Viceroy of India, Lord Hardinge, in 1916. The campus was designed like half a wheel, with interlinking arcs of buildings and gardens. The faculties of philosophy, Sanskrit and others are well regarded and draw students from all parts of India.

On campus is the Bharat Kala Bhavan Museum, which originated from the private collection of Rai Krishnadasa. The museum has an assortment of objects that trace over 2,000 years of Banaras' unbroken history. The most ancient objects are the small but exquisite array of clay images that date from the 3rd century BC. There are also early examples of Buddhist art and Hindu stone sculptures. The galleries of sculptures are filled with art objects from various parts of India. On the walls are examples of painting from the 16-17th century and from the imperial court of the Mughals. These paintings do much to explain the life, arts and costumes of the medieval period in India, before the dominance of Western influences.

The Banaras region was administered by Hindu rulers for several hundred years until the 17th century, when it fell into the hands of the Mughals. Following the practices of the times, many buildings of the previous rulers and the religious structures of the Hindus and Buddhists were demolished during the wars of conquest. In Banaras there are many sites where a temple once stood and where now a mosque or some other structure stands. However, there is a little known *farman*, or royal decree, in the most beautiful calligraphy, in the Bharat Kala Bhavan museum, which claims that Aurangzeb, the last great Mughal ruler, ordered his administrators to refrain from destroying any more temples. In subsequent years, as Banaras continued its haphazard growth, those temples that were destroyed were either rebuilt or relocated.

There are many ways of seeing Banaras. A walk through the lanes and markets offers a treat for the senses. There is colour everywhere and the fragrance of food cooking on open ovens. The crowded markets sell everything from trinkets to car parts. Around the temples there are always shops selling objects used for rituals. Each deity has his or her favorite flowers, which devotees offer in worship. Garlands, incense and camphor are sold along with offerings of sweets and sugar candy. In the cantonment area and on the roads from the railway station, one can see remnants of the British raj in the colonial architecture and layout of the gardens.

In the past, Banaras could met the needs of its inhabitants and the annual influx of pilgrims but is now so congested that it finds it hard to cope just with its inhabitants. Efforts to preserve this ancient city are being undertaken by voluntary and government projects. There is a programme to clean the entire length of the Ganga, and river turtles and fish have been reintroduced into the waters to deal with the excessive matter that is constantly being thrown into it. INTACH (The Indian National Trust for Art and Cultural Heritage) and the Ganga Action Plan are also monitoring the disposal of sewage and industrial waste in the river. Their efforts have made an enormous difference, though the pressure on the facilities and amenities is growing every day.

Since Banaras is a pilgrimage centre, respected and honoured throughout India, pilgrims come from every corner of the country. Some travel 2,000 kilometres (1,250 miles) to bathe in the Ganga and to honour their dead. Earlier pilgrims walked to Banaras on foot, usually visiting other pilgrimage centres along the way. The antiquity of Banaras is known not merely by archeological remains but by the diverse literature of India. At Banaras you still see people from all parts of the country in their native clothes, talking and chattering in their regional languages. In many ways it was pilgrimages to places such as Banaras that united the peoples of this

A little child dressed up for a festive occasion, with a brocade hat with tassels. It is customary for children to wear black kohl around their eyes and a black beauty spot to ward off the evil eye.

Contemplating the sunset of one's life

diverse country. At the pilgrimage centres they learnt about the customs and ideas of other pilgrims. They also learnt of different lands and strange new places. Crisscrossing the country, these pilgrims-together with traveling mendicants and theatre companies-disseminated the rich culture, mythology and philosophy of India. Despite the warring kings who ruled over separate Indian kingdoms, they united the length and breadth of the subcontinent.

When travellers come to Banaras, they stay in ashrams and rest houses, some specially favoured by one community or group. Throughout the city's history its rulers' have always permitted people from other states to visit and perform their religious duties-perhaps because there were taxes to be collected and money to be made from the stream of visitors that came. Shops with items that pilgrims need have grown around the temples. The *pandas*, or professional priests, have become an establishment at Banaras. They see to the needs of the pilgrims, telling them how to conduct the rites. As the pilgrims come from different parts of the country some *pandas* speak several regional Indian languages, while others specialize in the varying rites performed by different communities.

With the influx of pilgrims, Banaras developed as a trade centre. Apart from traders, crafts people also settled in Banaras. Today the city is famed for its silk weavers, who prepare the finest types of woven silk fabrics. A Banaras silk sari or shawl is traditionally a single coloured textile with motifs and patterns woven in gold or silver threads. The technique is complicated and demands great expertise. As the warp and the weft are interwoven on the loom, small, often minute shuttles with gold thread are introduced to form the motif. When the design of the motif is completed, a knot is made and the gold thread cut. The weaving continues until the next design. The smaller the motif or the more intricate the design, the more complex the weaving skills required. Silk weaving in Banaras is a cottage industry and in many areas of the city, especially the Muslim quarters, one can see looms set up in people's homes. Inside dim-lit rooms, the entire space is occupied by looms that heave and sigh all day long. The whole family is involved, and often children learn the art from their elders at a very young age. There are shops in Banaras, and throughout India, that sell these fine silk fabrics.

Perhaps one of the most heart-warming aspects of Banaras, as in other parts of the country, is the way people of different religions work in harmony, especially during the celebration of festivals. At Banaras, every day is said to be a special occasion, a temple festival or an event. This is not surprising as there are thousands of shrines, each with their unique calendar of events. The months of January and February herald the end of the cold months. On a moonless night between February and March *Shivratri*, the great night of Shiva, is celebrated. Devotees fast throughout the day and offer thanksgiving at Shiva temples, like the Visvanatha Temple. It is believed by some that the great pillar of light that proved Shiva's supremacy over Vishnu and Brahma appeared on *Shivratri*.

With the beginning of the new Hindu month of Chaitra, between March and April, the joy of spring fills the air. On the festival of Holi, coloured powder and paint are thrown into the air, or over relatives and friends, in an attempt to capture the colours of spring and the season of renewal. This is followed by the nine-day celebration of the goddess. Banaras has some very ancient shrines dedicated to manifestations of the female powers. There is the Chausat yogini shrine, dedicated to the 64 *yoginis* or manifestations of Sakti, the goddess of fertility, growth and prosperity. Others to the powers against illness and diseases, Shitala devi and to Lakshmi, the goddess of bounty and prosperity. As in life, so also in the manifestations of the gods, all aspects of life and death are acknowledged and respected.

During summer, the snows begin to melt in the distant Himalayas and later during the monsoon the River Ganga at Banaras swells and rises as thousands gather to bathe in her holy waters. August and September are the months when festivities, processions and decorations mark the special days of Ganesh, the Lord of Good Fortune and the Remover of Obstacles. The birthday of Krishna, the cow herd incarnation of Vishnu, is celebrated on Krishna Janmashtami.

The cooler months of October and November are the best time to be in Banaras. There are several festivals during this period, including the *Navratras* (nine auspicious nights) and the celebration of *Dussehra*. This festival lasts for ten days and is linked to the worship of the goddess and the story of Ram, an incarnation of Vishnu. There are many versions of this story, but the best known is found in the epic poem called the *Ramayana*. It is the story of a prince called Ram who was exiled from his kingdom because of jealousy and court politics. He was forced to leave his princely home in the company of his faithful wife, Sita, and brother, Lakshman. The story then narrates the 14 years of exile in the forest and the adventures and trials that they faced. In the forest, Sita was abducted and taken away by the ten-headed King Ravan of Lanka. The fight then began between good and evil. Ram, with the assistance of Lakshman and the monkey army of Hanuman, eventually found Sita and destroyed the forces of Ravan. The *Ramayana* ends with the triumphant return of Ram, Sita and Lakshman to their rightful kingdom.

This entire story is enacted and relived on the streets of Banaras. There are several places where the drama takes place, the most famous of which are the Ramnagar fort and Chitrakoot. Here, young boys play the parts of Ram, Sita and Lakshman and are ornately decorated with costumes and tinsel makeup. The city is the backdrop for much of the play (*lila*). It is through the streets that Ram walks when he is exiled from his kingdom. It is in them that the forest scenes are enacted. When the final battle takes place, huge paper-and-bamboo effigies filled with fire crackers are set alight to celebrate the death of Ravan and all that is evil. The Ramnagar *Ramlila* was at one time patronized by the royal family of Banaras. Even today the ex-Raja of Banaras attends the celebrations riding on an elephant. He supports the festivities with donations to the musicians and actors.

The *Ramlila* is not merely a play with actors and audience; it is total theatre. The whole audience participates, joining the chorus and moving with the actors to different venues as the story unfolds. It is prayer in action on a grand scale. There are few who are able to remain uninvolved in the festival of *Dussehra*. Most of the elaborate headgear and costumes and even the effigies for the Ramlila are made by expert Muslim artists. The audience comprises all age groups and denominations; some will be seeing the spectacle for the first time, while others will have seen the production every year of their lives.

The festival of lights, or *Divali*, follows soon after, commemorating the happy homecoming of Ram. Everywhere in India houses are lit with lights, oil lamps and gaudy electric bulbs. Lights are put on windows and doorways, and along parapets and balconies to enable Ram to find his way home to the hearts of his devotees. It is the festival of good fortune; people clean and decorate their homes to entice Lakshmi, the Goddess of Wealth and Prosperity, to enter their homes.

Finally, there is *Kartik Purnima* in November. On this lovely night the river Ganga glows and moonbeams flicker on her eternal waves. Thousands of pilgrims gather to celebrate the full moon. It is an occasion to commemorate the dead by lighting lamps beside her holy waters. Paper lamps are strung on tall bamboo poles and arranged by the waters' edge to brighten the way for the dead. It is a blessed night, one of the most auspicious at Banaras, and it encapsulates the mystery of this holy city.

Sun worship has ancient roots in India. There are a number of shrines dedicated to Surya, the sun god, in northern India and in Banaras. Water is a central part of sun worship and all sun temples are built near a river, lake or sea or with an adjoining tank.

Preceding pages
Every mood of the city of Banaras can be cherished. As the day fades, the lingering colours of the sunset dissolve into darkness and beside the river only ribbons of light can be seen as people carry lamps for the evening rituals.

There are a number of nineteenth century prints, drawings, paintings and written accounts of Banaras by early European visitors. From all accounts it appears as though little has changed in the intervening century. The skyline, the bathing and cremation ghats still dominate the river bank.

Those who have renounced the world and fulfilled all their earthly duties take spiritual asylum at Banaras. There is a certain pace and rhythm in the life of Banaras which is punctuated by personal rituals and public festivals.

Opposite page
Flower offerings are made to the river Ganga and to ancestors whose ashes have been immersed at Banaras. Flower sellers bring their wares in huge baskets to the riverside. Marigolds, garlands of many flowers and small clay oil lamps are sold as offerings to the pilgrims.

Religious gurus and mendicant sadhus, who have renounced the world of earthly pleasures, come to Banaras to pray, meditate and discuss philosophy. Their attire, headdress and the vermillion and ash powder markings on the forehead indicate their religious leanings. The large 'V' mark with a line in the middle is the symbol of the worshipper of Vishnu, the Preserver and Sustainer of the universe. Three broad horizontal lines across the forehead indicate a Shiva-bhakt or those who worship Shiva, the Creator and Destroyer.

Even for the local inhabitants the river is not just a place to have a bath or a convenient place to swim in the hot summer months. For them, as well as the pilgrims who travel from great distances, this is the most sacred of all places.

Right
Boats are taken to mid-stream to immerse the ashes of the dead. A boat ride at sunrise and at the gentle light of sunset offers the best panoramic view of Banaras' historic and sacred riverside.

Boats, ferries and cargo vessels ply the waterfront bringing vital supplies and pilgrims to their destination.

Water is one of the five elements that constitute the universe, from where life first emerges and to which it returns at death. Water worship is central to the theme and religious significance of Banaras. Holy water from the Ganga called "Ganga-jal" is sold in containers to pilgrims to carry home for rituals.

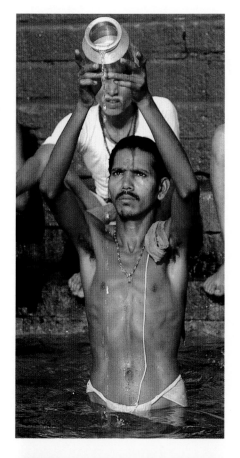

Prayer by the river is a private and personal experience and everyone has their own particular and individual form of expression. For some the day begins at dawn with the worship of the sun, the great source of energy, and then the waters, that sustain life on earth.

Banaras will never grow old as each successive generation returns to the city and the holy waters of the Ganga, to honour their ancestors. Some come each year to conduct these rituals, others when they can. Widows and the aged ,who no longer have family responsibilities come to the peaceful, scholarly and sacred sanctuary of Banaras to spend their last few years.

Opposite page
A charming sight along the riverside are the large bamboo poles placed specifically to serve as a perch for birds. Buddhists, Jains and Hindus put an inspiring accent on service in their religious rituals and practices. Good deeds, are suggested as part of worship, not merely for the benefit of our fellow humans but also for the birds, animals and insects on whom the survival of human-life depends.

For the foreign visitor to India, riverside activity is often an unexpected experience, a strange and yet casual mixture of the sacred and the profane.

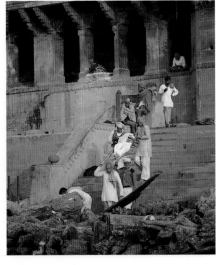

Opposite page
Banaras is the city of death and is also the city of life and re-birth, of joy and sorrow. Life, in the city, does not stop but goes on despite the constant reminder that death is an inevitable part of life.

At the cremation grounds a corpse is laid to rest on the funeral pyre. There is a traditional community, the Doms, who manage and supervise the cremation grounds and ghats.

Every city has its moods. Most people like the gentle hours of dawn by the riverside or rich colours the sun casts on the ancient monuments of Banaras. Day time is for work and toil, as women paddle their boats across the river. The tranquility of the river is disturbed only during the summer, with monsoon rains when the rising floods carrying silt and debris erode the banks, toppling embankments and swallowing up portions of the land.

Opposite page
The most important shrine at Banaras is the Visvanatha temple dedicated to Shiva, the "Lord of all". This temple today houses a linga, a stone non-figurative image, a mark of Shiva. It has been reconstructed several times since the 17th century and the gold-plating on the roof was donated to the Visvanatha temple by the great sikh ruler, Maharaja Ranjit Singh.

As the pilgrims return from their ritual bath, and make their way to the temple for prayer, they give alms to the poor, and buy idols and trinkets for the home. Banaras attracts pilgrims from all parts of India and is therefore also the melting pot of Indian culture.

Opposite page
*Though Shiva is the presiding deity of Banaras,
there are several shrines to local deities and
other goddesses and gods of the hindu pantheon.*

*Along the river-front, the ghats and the small
lanes are crowded with street hawkers selling
ritual flower and sweet offerings, religious
posters and souvenirs for the pilgrims to take
home and toys for children.*

The Shiv-linga stands on a base called the "yoni" which symbolizes the female principle while the ling represents the 'formless' most supreme source of creation. Worship with water, flower and fruit offerings are accompanied by the ringing of bells and the arati, when lamps are lit to symbolize that the light of spiritual knowledge is being evoked to dispel the darkness of ignorance.

Banaras is the home of millions of deities and almost every day of the year is an occasion for celebration. The festival of Durga Puja is celebrated each year in the months of October and November. Durga, Mother of the Universe and consort of Shiva, is one of the most important female deities of the hindu pantheon. She is also called Kali, the dark and terrible one, or Gauri, the fair young virgin. Each of her countless names represent the myriad manifestations of the great goddess.

The busy streets of Banaras can no longer cope with the ever increasing migration of pilgrims and the swelling local population. Every so often even a corpse gets stuck in a traffic jam!

Cycle rickshaws are the cheapest mode of transport and everyone from over-dressed veiled women in purdah to 'under-dressed' tourists use these human machines. A large percentage of Indians do not have their own vehicles, those that do always end up transporting one too many.

Shops are often portable stalls with objects for sale laid on the ground, suspended from sticks or umbrellas or just carried by hand. The permanent shops tend to sell an assortment of wares, tightly packed into narrow shelves.

An Indian market is incomplete without the open foodstalls, selling freshly fried snacks, savoury samosas and sweet meats. Shops remain open till late evening, for the benefit of working people. Shop keepers sit and chat while waiting for the potential custom. Once a buyer is spotted they begin their hard sales drive, enthsiastically claiming that they have things for sale that you would not find anywhere else in the world.

The narrow streets of Banaras are also the scene of street entertainment and theatrical performances. The artists announce their performances with heavy drumming and song.

Near Banaras is the famous carpet weaving centre at Bhadoi where handmade carpets are produced by skilled craftsmen who have acquired their rich repertoire of designs and techniques from their ancestral traditions.

Banaras also is famous for its silk weaving cottage industry. The process of weaving silk begins with the making of the yarn, then rolling it on to a spindle, a job that requires very dexterous fingers and so the entire family is involved in creative work.

Large looms are set up in the home, with an elaborate frame for the warp and weft threads. Banarsi silk brocades have small, often minute, motifs made of gold or silver thread. Each motif has to be created individually using tiny shuttles. In the old days the gold thread was authentic, but today artificial fibres are used.

Opposite page
Hidden amidst the tangle of crowded over-built areas are the historical buildings. Islamic arches, colonial administrative buildings and native houses all co-exist in close proximity to each other.

Below left
In the Observatory, built by Maharaja Jai Singh II of Jaipur in the18th century, these large strangely modern forms were used as sundials, clocks and very efficient instruments to chart the movement of the sun and the other planets.

Below right
Banaras is an ancient city, built and re-built over several centuries. Its varied and eventful history is recorded in a wonderful assortment of architectural styles and form.

Left
Detail of the Nepali Temple constructed by the King of Nepal early this century. The sloping roof, wooden door and window frames are of characteristic Nepalese design.

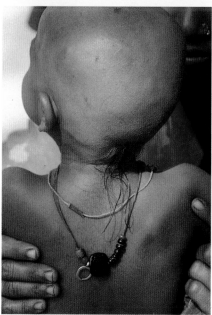

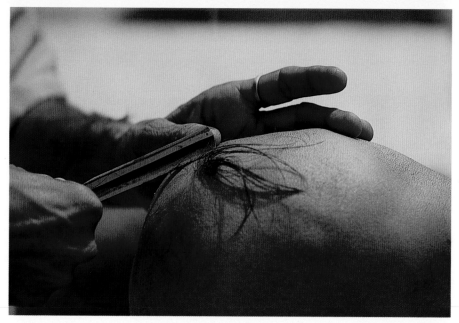

Banaras is a recognized home of learning and religious education and still attracts students who wish to study philosophy, sanskrit and the traditional sciences, like homeopathy and natural medicine or Ayurveda.

The Banaras Hindu University
was established in the early 20th
century to preserve and perpetuate
traditional Indian education and to
counterbalance the influence of the
British educational system. The
University, the brain child of
Pandit Malviya, has a temple
and Bharat Kala Museum on
its campus.

At Sarnath, near Banaras, a few
5th-6th century stupas and
remains of monasteries mark the
vererated site.

Opposite page
Above
*The Dhamek stupa, commemorates the historic visit of the Buddha. The
stupa or funerary mound is decorated with low relief scrolls of flowers
and leaves. The Archelogical Survey Museum has a collection of objects
excavated at Sarnath, including the lion capital of Emperor Ashok, 3rd
century B.C. which was later adopted as the symbol of the Indian republic.*
Below
*Devotees from all nations come to Sarnath to study and pray at one of the
holiest of Buddhist sites.*

Preceeding pages
Life in the city of Banaras is sustained by the produce from neighbouring villages which is brought to huge, very colourful markets.

Local vegetables and fruit are brought early morning and sold on the streets. Villagers sell to retailers and the market place resound with the sounds of bargaining customers and anxious farmers.

Beyond Banaras, the Indian countryside is gentle and tranquil in contrast to the bustling sound of the holy city. Women tend to work much harder than the men for their families.

All roads seem to lead to Banaras and on festive occasions they are lined with carts carrying families into the city for the celebrations.

Wherever the festivites take place a temporary market is set up to meet the demands of the pilgrims. Rows and rows of tiny painted clay, plaster cast and papier mâche images compete for the attention of the devotee. The celebrations also attract the participation of ritual performers, who dress up and gather alms in the name of their patron deity.

Above
Hijras, transvestites dressed up in garish female attire also join in. Their presence is considered auspicious and they collect alms from those who are celebrating a marriage or a birth.

More than half the population of India's children do not have the privilege of going to school or completing their school education. They spend their time helping the family in collecting water and firewood, looking after the cattle and playing with their siblings. Efforts of the government and numerous voluntary agencies have made considerable gains in ensuring that all children have their share of childhood joys and receive their rightful claims of nutrition, protection, health and education.

Opposite page

Pilgrims follow different rituals at Banaras. The most popular is the ritual walk or Panchkroshi to visit the 108 shrines around the city over a period of several days and nights.

Many people undertake a ritual as part of a vow that precedes or follows the fulfillment of a wish or prayer. The deities worshipped range from local ones to goddesses that protect against illness, tree spirits and the forces of nature.

Banaras was once ruled by its Maharaja. Today, in the world's largest democracy, the role of the ex-Maharaja is restricted to special occasions. The ex-Maharaja is still the patron of this annual celebration.

Opposite page
The Ramnagar fort on the banks of the river is the scene of the annual Ramlila ritual performance which falls between the months of October and November.

The Ramlila is a quasi-religious theatre performance based on the story of Rama, the hero-god of the epic poem Ramayana, where he, his wife Sita and brother Lakshmana were forced in to exile. During their trials in the forest Hanuman, the Lord of the monkeys, comes to their help. Sita was kidnapped by Ravana, the lustful King of Lanka.

The enactment of the Ramlila continues for several nights, and the climax is reached when the gigantic effigy of Ravan burnt, amidst fireworks displays and rejoicement that evil has been conquered goodness, virtue and heroism.

An A To Z of Facts and Figures

ASHRAM, A retreat, usually run by a religious association, offering a resting place for pilgrims, students and those belonging to a particular religious order. Banaras has several ashrams for visiting pilgrims.

BHADHOI, 74 kilometres (46 miles) from Banaras, is famed as a carpet centre. The ancient carpet industry of India has been influenced by the workmanship of Persia, Kashmir and the Far East. Today, there are factories and workshops that manufacture pile and woven carpets, in silk, wool and cotton. Many of them are exported, and many of the designs and colours of the carpets have been adapted to the Western market. Carpets from Bhadhoi can be ordered and posted to any address around the world.

CHAUKHANDI, is the brick terraced temple at Sarnath that marks the spot where the Buddha delivered his first sermon. The brick temple is a Gupta construction from the 4th-6th century. Within the Sarnath complex there are many structures that have been built and rebuilt in different historical periods. Today, there is a thriving Buddhist monastery and craft centre at Sarnath, which meets the needs of visiting Buddhist pilgrims.

DASHASHVAMEDHA GHAT, One of the most important ghats in Banaras, built by Peshwa Balaji Baji Rao. The name is derived from a myth of the ten (*das*) *ashvamedha* (horse sacrifices) conducted by Lord Brahma. There are several shrines located here, including that of the goddess Shitala. The stairs of the ghat lead down to the river and many believe that a bath at the Dashashvemedha Ghat is the high point of their pilgrimage.

ELEPHANT, The elephant is one of India's most respected and loved animals. Its immense size and stature have earned it a place in Hindu mythology as the carrier of the world, the mount of Indra, the Lord of the Sky. It is thus used in all religious processions. The elephant was the regal mount for earthly kings as well as the gods: during the *Dussehra* celebrations the ex-Maharaja of Banaras rides through the town on an elephant.

FARMAN, A royal decree that records the instructions of the rulers of the kingdom. The Bharat Kala Bhavan has a few of the famous *farman* of the Mughal rulers. They are written in exquisite calligraphy in the arabic-persian script and carry the seal of the emperor.

GANESH, is the elephant-headed son of Lord Shiva. He is the Lord of Wisdom and leader of Shiva's army of *ganas*. As Remover of Obstacles, he is worshipped at the commencement of every new venture, journey and undertaking. Conventional images, with large flapping ears and long trunk, can be seen throughout Banaras. The Bharat Kala Bhavan museum has some beautiful medieval sculptures of the dancing Ganesh.

HUIEN TSANG, A Chinese traveller who visited India in the seventh century. His accounts provide important historical descriptions of famous Buddhist sites, including Banaras (or Polonisse as he called it), where he saw a thriving religious centre and over 30 monasteries. A constant flow of pilgrims and students from the Far East, from ancient times to the present, has ensured that contact with the famous Buddhist sites has been maintained. They still come to view the original Buddhist sites, to study, to see the original stupas and to worship there.

INDIAN MUSIC, Banaras is famed for its musical tradition and is the home and grooming ground of several of India's great musicians. Ustad Bismillah Khan the renowned Shenai (a wind instrument) player, and Pundit Ravi Shanker, who made the sitar (a stringed instrument) famous throughout the world, have both adopted Banaras as their home. Many students come to Banaras to study with these ustad and maestros.

JNANA VAPI MOSQUE, is so called because it was founded on the ruins of the Visvanatha Temple. Aurangzeb, the Mughal emperor, had this large mosque constructed in the 17th century. As was the practice in the medieval period, carved stones and slabs were used in the construction of the mosque. The mosque follows the plan of all Islamic religious buildings with a *mirab*, an alcove, to indicate the westerly direction of Mecca, to which all the devotees must face while praying. The mosque has towering minarets, or *minars*, which the priest used to climb five times a day to call the devoted to prayer. The proximity of the mosque to the temple complex makes the area a busy pilgrimage centre.

KARTIKKEYA, Another son of Shiva. He is depicted on works of art riding a peacock and is the lord of Shiva's army. In one version of the myth he was born of Shiva's seed, carried away by Agni (Lord of the Fire) and brought up by the Ganga. The Bharat Kala Bhavan museum has a 5th-century Gupta sculpture of Kartikkeya from the Banaras region. He is seated on a peacock whose beautiful tail is spread like a halo behind him.

LALITHA GHAT, This popular bathing area is between the Mir and Manikarnika ghats. It is famous for the Vishnu temple called Ganga Keshava and a shrine to the river goddess Bhagirathi Devi. Also nearby is a 19th-century Nepali temple. The building was made under the patronage of Rajendra Bir Vikram Shah of Nepal and is characterized by its wooden window and door frames.

MANIKARNIKA GHAT, This is the most important ghat and *tirth* on the river. Pilgrims bathe here before they visit the Visvanatha Temple, the centre of the pilgrimage to Banaras. The myth tells how the sweat of Vishnu's austerities filled the lake. Another story narrates how Parvati's jewelled (*mani*) earring (*karnika*) fell into the *kund*, the lake, while she was bathing here.

NAGA PANCHMI, On this festival, which falls during the monsoon season, snakes are worshipped, homes are decorated with paintings and images are propitiated with food offerings. Snake worship is still prevalent today. Snakes are associated with water, the underworld, and hence fertility. Farmers throughout the country, especially in southern India, worship snakes because they are aware of the helpful role that snakes play in agriculture.

OM, A mystical sound pronounced 'Aum'. It is written on the walls of the temples, and on various religious items. It is believed that this is the original sound that accompanied the creation of the world, and is used in meditation and chanting as a means to return to that original source within.

OBSERVATORY, The observatory is near the Dashashvamedha and the Man Mandir ghats. It was built by the scientist Maharaja Jai Singh II, the ruler of Jaipur. The strange, contemporary looking structures were constructed in 1710. They were used as accurate sun dials and clocks and to plot the movement of the planets and stars. Similar observatories were constructed by Jai Singh in his royal capital of Jaipur, and in Delhi and Ujjain.

PANCHKROSHI, The sequence and form of worship conducted by the pilgrims has a special significance. The *panchkroshi* is a circular path that begins at the Manikarnika ghat. The *panchkroshi* takes five days with four night stops. There are 108 places of worship en route where the pilgrims offer prayers.

QUEEN HOLKAR, or Rani Ahilya Bai Holkar of Indore (now in the state of Madhya Pradesh), had the Visvanatha Temple rebuilt for the third time in 1776. It was customary for royal families to invest in temple construction in the sacred city, and many prominent buildings and ghats were donated by the royal houses of central and western India.

RAMNAGAR The tall bastions of the Ramnagar fort can be seen on the banks of the Ganga, opposite and upstream from Banaras. The 17th-century fort, 16 kilometres (10 miles) away from Banaras, was the home of the Maharaja; now a small part of it serves as a public museum. During the *Dussehra* festival in October-November, it forms the backdrop for the enactment of the *Ramlila*.

SURYA, The Lord of the Sun is worshipped in Banaras at many sites and at many festivals. The Lolarka *kund*, located in the southern corner of the city, is one of the most ancient sites for sun worship in India. Surya is worshipped for the cures of leprosy and other illnesses, and to ensure general good health.

TIRTH, This literally means the 'crossing over' and refers to the pilgrimage to holy sites on the river. The act of cleansing and bathing by the pilgrims is a symbolic gesture of spiritual cleansing to ensure that life may start anew. There are lists available of the important tirth sites of India, and this mythological geography binds the country together.

UTTARA KASHI, In Hindu cosmology, Kashi of Banaras is considered the holiest centre of the earth. It is, therefore, not unusual to find places that imitate the same name. Northern Kashi, or Uttara Kashi, is on the Ganga in the Garhwal Himalayas and has become a holy pilgrimage site with temples named after those in Banaras.

WORSHIP, consists of special rituals and ceremonies. *Puja*, meaning worship, is the offering of flowers to honour the deity. *Prasad*, divine grace, refers to the food offered to the deity and then fed to the devotees as sanctified, consecrated blessings. *Darshan* meaning to be in the presence of the Almighty, refers to the sight or glimpse of the deity when you visit the temple.

YOGA, One of many ways to gain enlightenment, yoga is a system of concentration and disciplined living, involving control over the physical and mental levels of existence, thereby promoting self-awareness and the power to be at peace with oneself. Yoga as a method has evolved specific and elaborate combinations of physical exercises and breath control practices to strengthen the body's powers to cleanse and cure itself.

About the Photographer:

Pankaj Shah originally took up photography as a means of recording his social work in India, Africa, Europe and the Middle East. In 1977 he decided to become a professional photographer after his pictures were published in the *Daily Mail* and *Evening Standard* of London. Since then he has had over 200 magazine covers to his credit and his pictures have been published worldwide. He is busy establishing — *Resource Foto* — an indian picture library and working on a book entitled *Performing Art of Kerala*. He contributed to *Our World in Colour Khajuraho*, published by The Guidebook Company in1991.

About the author:

Shobita Punja was born in South India and attended several schools in India, Beirut and London. She has degrees in History and the History of Art from the Jawaharlal Nehru University in Delhi, and one in Art Education from Stanford University in California. She has travelled extensively in the course of her studies, and is presently engaged lecturing both students and teachers with the aim of 'creating an appreciation for the rich cultural heritage of India'. She is the author of *Museums of India*, 1989, and *Khajuraho*, 1991, both published by the Guidebook Company and *Divine Ecstasy—The Story of Khajuraho*, 1992, published by Viking.

GS/68/01